The Urbana Free Library

To renew: call **217-367-4057**
or go to **urbanafreelibrary.org**
and select **My Account**

Bulldozers ✦ Buldóceres

By/Por ERIN FALLIGANT

Illustrated by/Ilustrado por SR. SÁNCHEZ

Music by/Música por MARK OBLINGER

CANTATA
LEARNING

WWW.CANTATALEARNING.COM

CANTATA LEARNING

Published by Cantata Learning
1710 Roe Crest Drive
North Mankato, MN 56003
www.cantatalearning.com

Library of Congress Cataloging-in-Publication Data
Names: Falligant, Erin, author. | Sanchez, Sr., 1973– illustrator. |
  Oblinger, Mark, composer. | Falligant, Erin. Bulldozers. | Falligant,
  Erin. Bulldozers. Spanish.
Title: Bulldozers / by Erin Falligant ; illustrated by Sr. Sanchez ; music by
  Mark Oblinger = Buldoceres / por Erin Falligant ; ilustrado por Sr.
  Sanchez ; musica por Mark Oblinger.
Other titles: Buldoceres
Description: North Mankato, MN : Cantata Learning, [2019] | Series: Machines!
  = Las maquinas! | Includes bibliographical references. | Audience: Ages
  6–7. | Audience: Grades K to 3. | Text in English and Spanish.
Identifiers: LCCN 2018026140 (print) | LCCN 2018029842 (ebook) | ISBN
  9781684103577 (eBook) | ISBN 9781684103379 (hardcover) | ISBN
  9781684103737 (pbk.)
Subjects: LCSH: Earthwork--Juvenile literature. | Bulldozers--Juvenile
  literature.
Classification: LCC TA732 (ebook) | LCC TA732 .F35 2019 (print) | DDC
  629.225--dc23
LC record available at https://lccn.loc.gov/2018026140

Book design and art direction: Tim Palin Creative
Production assistance: Shawn Biner
Editorial direction: Kellie M. Hultgren
Music direction: Elizabeth Draper
Music arranged and produced by Mark Oblinger

Printed in the United States of America.
0397

ACCESS THE MUSIC!
SCAN CODE WITH MOBILE APP
CANTATALEARNING.COM

TIPS TO SUPPORT LITERACY AT HOME

Daily reading and singing with your child are fun and easy ways to build early literacy and language development.

USING CANTATA LEARNING BOOKS AND SONGS DURING YOUR DAILY STORY TIME

1. As you sing and read, point out the different words on the page that rhyme.

2. Memorize simple rhymes such as Itsy Bitsy Spider and sing them together.

3. Use the critical thinking questions in the back of each book to guide your singing and storytelling.

4. Follow the notes and words in the included sheet music with your child while you listen to the song.

5. Access music by scanning the QR code on each Cantata book. You can also stream or download the music for free to your computer, smartphone, or mobile device.

Devoting time to daily reading shows that you are available for your child. Together, you are building language, literacy, and listening skills.

Have fun reading and singing!

CONSEJOS PARA APOYAR LA ALFABETIZACIÓN EN EL HOGAR

Leer y cantar diariamente con su hijo son maneras divertidas y fáciles de promover la alfabetización temprana y el desarrollo del lenguaje.

USO DE LIBROS Y CANCIONES DE CANTATA DURANTE SU TIEMPO DIARIO DE LECTURA DE CUENTOS

1. Mientras canta y lee, señale las diferentes palabras en la página que riman.

2. Memorice rimas simples como Itsy Bitsy Spider y cántenlas juntos.

3. Use las preguntas críticas para pensar en la parte posterior de cada libro para guiar su canto y relato del cuento.

4. Siga las notas y las palabras en la partitura de música incluida con su hijo mientras escuchan la canción.

5. Acceda la música al escanear el código QR en cada libro de Cantata. Además, puede transmitir o bajar la música gratuitamente a su computadora, teléfono inteligente o dispositivo móvil.

Dedicar tiempo a la lectura diaria muestra que usted está disponible para su hijo. Juntos, están desarrollando el lenguaje, la alfabetización y destrezas de comprensión auditiva.

¡Diviértanse leyendo y cantando!

A bulldozer is a powerful tractor. It pushes dirt and sand. It breaks up hard ground. It clears away trees and rocks. A bulldozer is so strong that it can push or pull other trucks!

To learn more about bulldozers, turn the page and sing along.

Un buldócer es un tractor poderoso. Empuja tierra y arena. Rompe el suelo duro. Despeja árboles y rocas. ¡Un buldócer es tan fuerte que puede empujar o tirar de otros camiones!

Para aprender más sobre los buldóceres, da vuelta la página y canta la canción.

What clears the way for roads and homes?
A big bulldozer can.
It pushes dirt and rocks away
so we can build again.

¿Qué hace camino para rutas y hogares?
Un buldócer grande puede hacerlo.
Empuja tierra y retira rocas
para que podamos construir de nuevo.

Rumble, rumble! Here it comes
through wind or snow or sun!
Bulldozers are the toughest trucks.
Their work is never done.

¡Qué retumbo! ¡Aquí viene,
a través del sol, nieve o viento!
El buldócer es el camión más fuerte.
Trabajar duro es su talento.

In back the **ripper** breaks the ground
with one tooth, two, or three.
In front, the **blade** will push the dirt
or even knock down trees.

Atrás el **escarificador** rompe la tierra
con uno, dos o tres dientes.
Al frente, la **cuchilla** empujará la tierra
o hasta algún árbol imponente.

Rumble, rumble! Here it comes
through wind or snow or sun!
Bulldozers are the toughest trucks.
Their work is never done.

¡Qué retumbo! ¡Aquí viene,
a través del sol, nieve o viento!
El buldócer es el camión más fuerte.
Trabajar duro es su talento.

Bulldozers move on heavy tracks
to help them get around.
They will not slip. They will not stop
on any kind of ground.

14

El buldócer se mueve sobre cadenas pesadas
para ayudarlo a desplazarse.
No resbalará ni se detendrá.
No logrará atascarse.

Rumble, rumble! Here it comes
through wind or snow or sun!
Bulldozers are the toughest trucks.
Their work is never done.

¡Qué retumbo! ¡Aquí viene,
a través del sol, nieve o viento!
El buldócer es el camión más fuerte.
Trabajar duro es su talento.

Bulldozers might work at a farm
or in a deep **landfill**.
What pushes heavy piles of trash?
A big bulldozer will!

Los buldóceres trabajan en granjas
o en un hondo **vertedero**.
¿Qué empuja pilas de basura?
¡Un buldócer verdadero!

Rumble, rumble! Here it comes
through wind or snow or sun!
Bulldozers are the toughest trucks.
Their work is never done.

¡Qué retumbo! ¡Aquí viene,
a través del sol, nieve o viento!
El buldócer es el camión más fuerte.
Trabajar duro es su talento.

SONG LYRICS
Bulldozers / Buldóceres

What clears the way for roads
and homes?
A big bulldozer can.
It pushes dirt and rocks away
so we can build again.

¿Qué hace camino para rutas
y hogares?
Un buldócer grande puede hacerlo.
Empuja tierra y retira rocas
para que podamos construir
de nuevo.

Rumble, rumble! Here it comes
through wind or snow or sun!
Bulldozers are the toughest trucks.
Their work is never done.

¡Qué retumbo! ¡Aquí viene,
a través del sol, nieve o viento!
El buldócer es el camión más fuerte.
Trabajar duro es su talento.

In back the ripper breaks the ground
with one tooth, two, or three.
In front, the blade will push the dirt
or even knock down trees.

Atrás el escarificador rompe la tierra
con uno, dos o tres dientes.

Al frente, la cuchilla empujará
la tierra
o hasta algún árbol imponente.

Rumble, rumble! Here it comes
through wind or snow or sun!
Bulldozers are the toughest trucks.
Their work is never done.

¡Qué retumbo! ¡Aquí viene,
a través del sol, nieve o viento!
El buldócer es el camión más fuerte.
Trabajar duro es su talento.

Bulldozers move on heavy tracks
to help them get around.
They will not slip. They will not stop
on any kind of ground.

El buldócer se mueve sobre cadenas
pesadas
para ayudarlo a desplazarse.
No resbalará ni se detendrá.
No logrará atascarse.

Rumble, rumble! Here it comes
through wind or snow or sun!
Bulldozers are the toughest trucks.
Their work is never done.

¡Qué retumbo! ¡Aquí viene,
a través del sol, nieve o viento!
El buldócer es el camión más fuerte.
Trabajar duro es su talento.

Bulldozers might work at a farm
or in a deep landfill.
What pushes heavy piles of trash?
A big bulldozer will!

Los buldóceres trabajan en granjas
o en un hondo vertedero.
¿Qué empuja pilas de basura?
¡Un buldócer verdadero!

Rumble, rumble! Here it comes
through wind or snow or sun!
Bulldozers are the toughest trucks.
Their work is never done.

¡Qué retumbo! ¡Aquí viene,
a través del sol, nieve o viento!
El buldócer es el camión más fuerte.
Trabajar duro es su talento.

Bulldozers / Buldóceres

Rock 'n' Roll
Mark Oblinger

Verse / Verso

1. What clears the way for roads and homes? A big bull-doz-er can. It push-es dirt and rocks a-way so we can build a-gain.

¿Qué ha-ce ca-mi-no pa-ra ru-tas y ho-ga-res? Un bul-dó-cer gran-de pue-de ha-cer-lo. Em-

pu-ja ti-e-rra y re-ti-ra ro-cas pa-ra que po-da-mos con-struir de nue-vo.

Chorus / Estribillo

Rum-ble, rum-ble! Here it comes through wind or snow or sun! Bull-doz-ers are the tough-est trucks. Their work is nev-er done.

¡Qué re-tum-bo! ¡A-quí vie-ne, a tra-vés del sol, ni-e-ve o vien-to! El bul-dó-cer es el ca-

mión más fuer-te. Tra-ba-jar du-ro es su ta-len-to.

Verse / Verso 2

In back the ripper breaks the ground
with one tooth, two, or three.
In front, the blade will push the dirt
or even knock down trees.

Atrás el escarificador rompe la tierra
con uno, dos o tres dientes.
Al frente, la cuchilla empujará la tierra
o hasta algún árbol imponente.

Chorus / Estribillo

Verse / Verso 3

Bulldozers move on heavy tracks
to help them get around.
They will not slip. They will not stop
on any kind of ground.

El buldócer se mueve sobre cadenas pesadas
para ayudarlo a desplazarse.
No resbalará ni se detendrá.
No logrará atascarse.

Chorus / Estribillo

Verse / Verso 4

Bulldozers might work at a farm
or in a deep landfill.
What pushes heavy piles of trash?
A big bulldozer will!

Los buldóceres trabajan en granjas
o en un hondo vertedero.
¿Qué empuja pilas de basura?
¡Un buldócer verdadero!

Chorus / Estribillo

GLOSSARY / GLOSARIO

blade—a metal plate that pushes or scoops
cuchilla—una placa de metal que empuja o levanta

landfill—a place where trash is buried in dirt
vertedero—un lugar donde se entierra la basura

ripper—a blade with teeth that break up hard ground
escarificador—una cuchilla con dientes que rompe el suelo duro

CRITICAL THINKING QUESTIONS

Where might you see bulldozers in your neighborhood? What might they be doing? Draw a picture of a bulldozer at work and write a sentence to describe what it is doing.

PREGUNTAS DE PENSAMIENTO CRÍTICO

¿Dónde podrías ver buldóceres en tu vecindario? ¿Qué podrían estar haciendo? Haz un dibujo de un buldócer trabajando y escribe una oración para describir lo que está haciendo.

FURTHER READING / OTROS LIBROS

Clay, Kathryn. *Bulldozers.* North Mankato, MN: Capstone, 2016.

Lennie, Charles. *Buldócers.* Minneapolis: Abdo Kids, 2014.

Osier, Dan. *Las Palas Mecánicas: Bulldozers.* New York, NY: PowerKids, 2014.

Schuh, Mari. *Bulldozers.* Mankato, MN: Amicus Ink, 2018..